Numbers Hidde

Color to find the hidden picture.

● = blue   ●● = yellow

This book belongs to

_____

Sandy Fun

These are fun to use in the sand.

Color to find the hidden pictures.

● = green   ●● = yellow

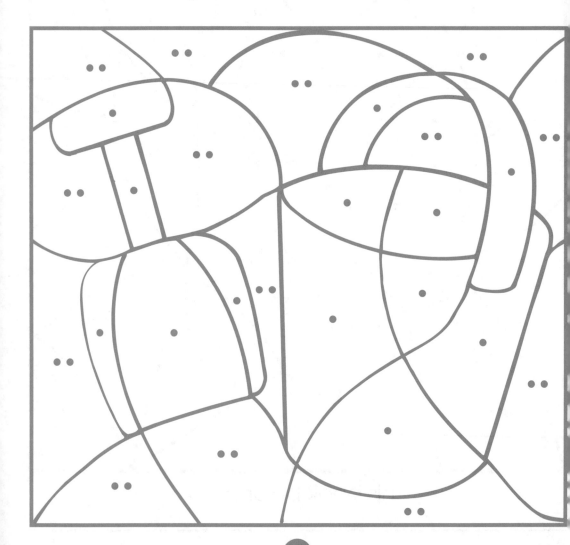

A Pretty Find

This can be found at the beach.

Color to find the hidden picture.

● ● = blue   ● ● ● = orange

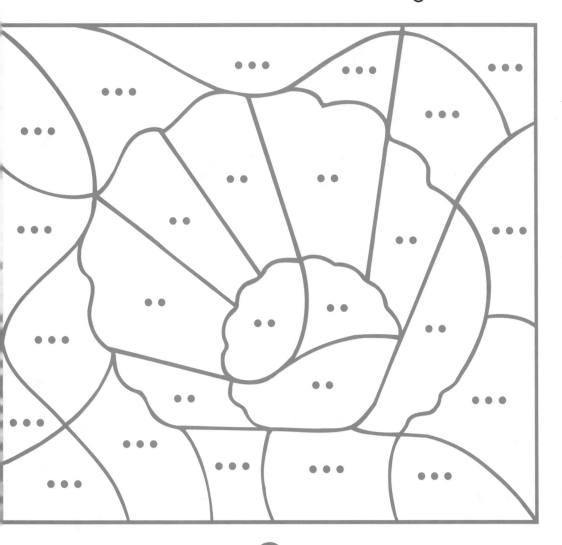

3

Always Home

This little animal carries its home on its back.

Color to find the hidden picture.

● ● = brown   ● ● ● = orange

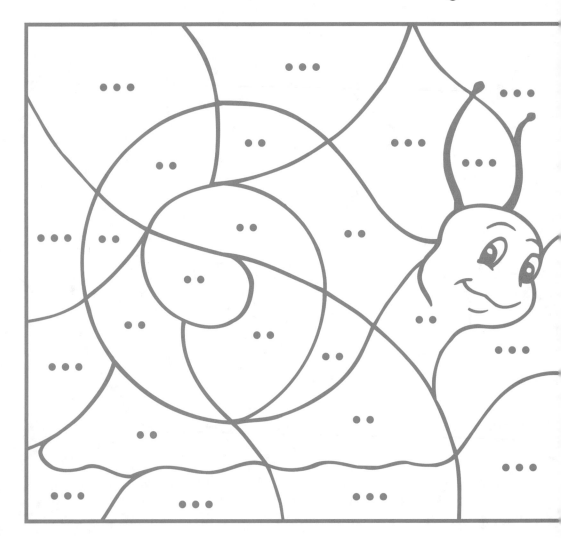

FS109006 • Numbers Hidden Picture

Watch It Twirl!

This is fun to watch in the wind.

Color to find the hidden picture.

● ● = green   = yellow

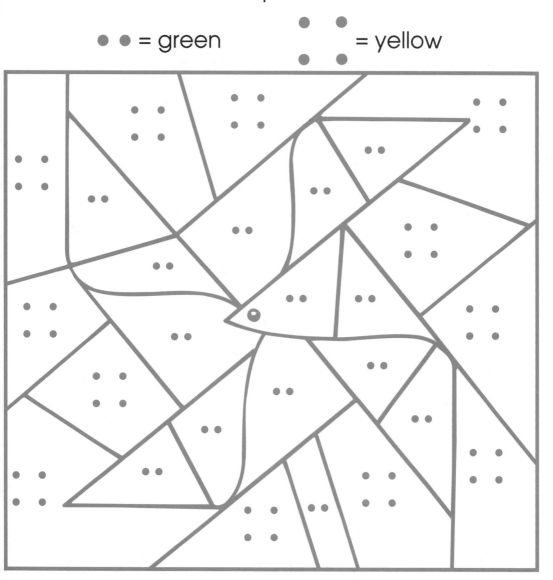

5

Rolling Along

You can glide around on this.

Color to find the hidden picture.

● ● ● = green   = blue

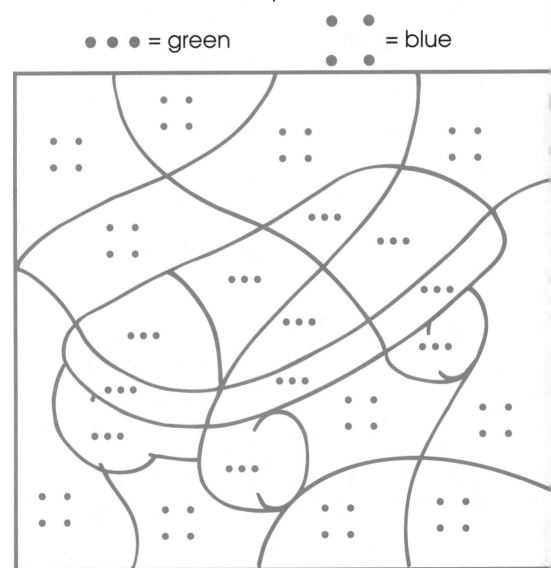

Let's Ride!

It is always fun to ride in this.

Color to find the hidden picture.

● ● ● = red   = yellow

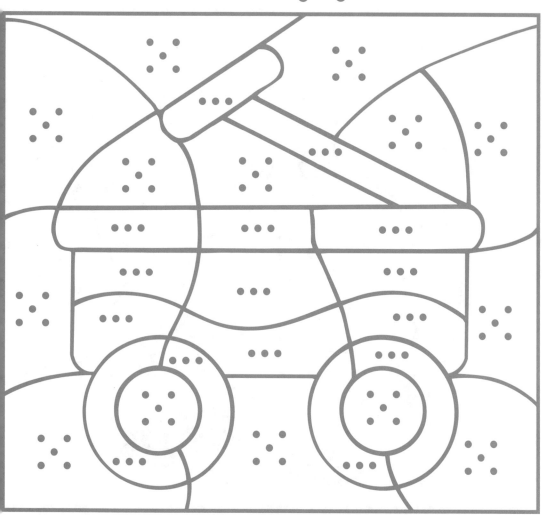

FS109006 • Numbers Hidden Pictures

Black and White

This striped animal can be found at the zoo.

Color to find the hidden picture.

= white   = red

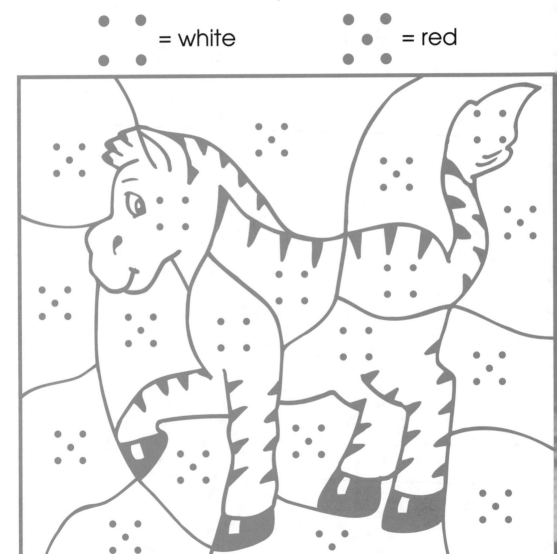

8

What a Lady!

This little bug is fun to hold.

Color to find the hidden picture.

= red   = yellow

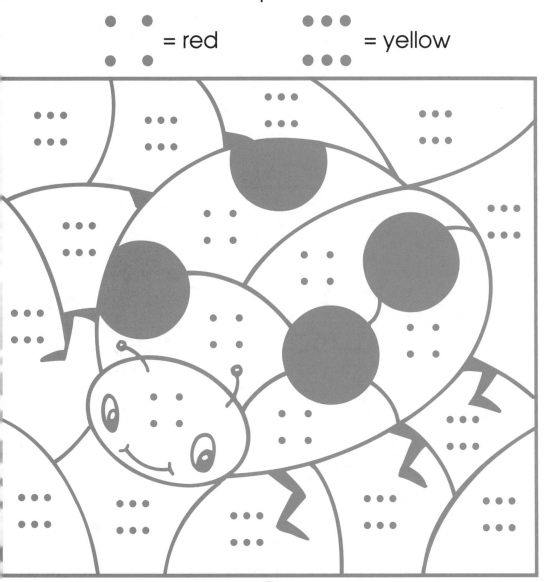

9

Sharp Enough to Cut

These are sure handy to have around.

Color to find the hidden picture.

= orange   = yellow

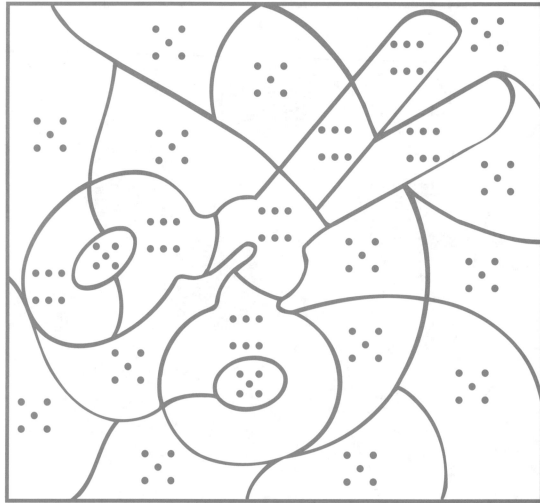

Here We Come!

People who put out fires ride on this.

Color to find the hidden picture.

= red = blue

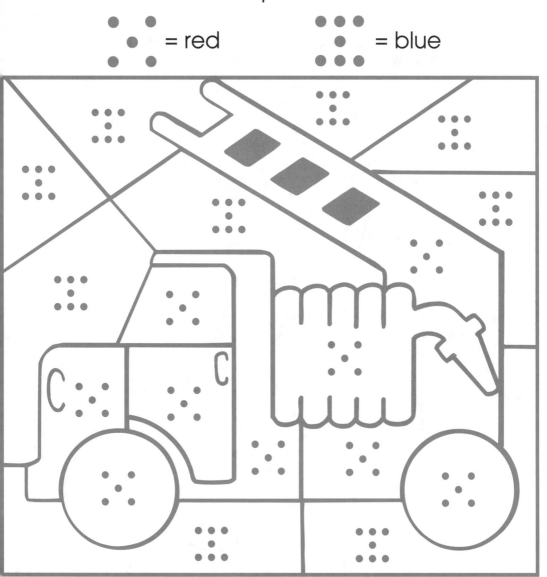

Away We Go!

Whee! This is fun to do at the park.

Color to find the hidden picture.

⋮⋮⋮ = pink   ⋮⋮⋮ = purple

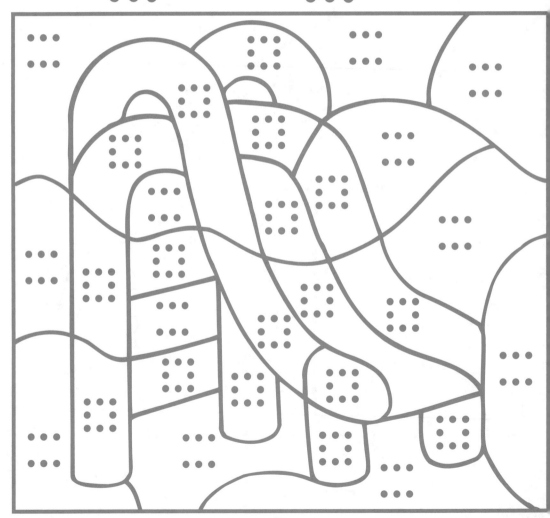

Push and Play

You can pretend to be a gardener.

Color to find the hidden picture.

= blue   = green

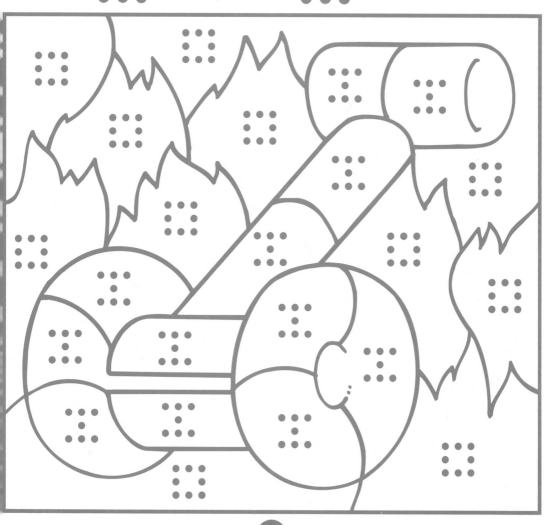

13

Let's Dance!

You might need these if you like to dance.

Color to find the hidden picture.

= pink   = yellow

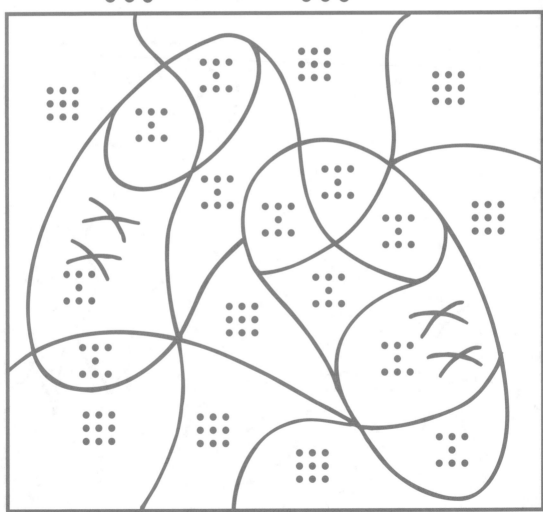

FS109006 • Numbers Hidden Pictures

A Big Cat

This animal can be seen at a zoo.

Color to find the hidden picture.

= orange   = green

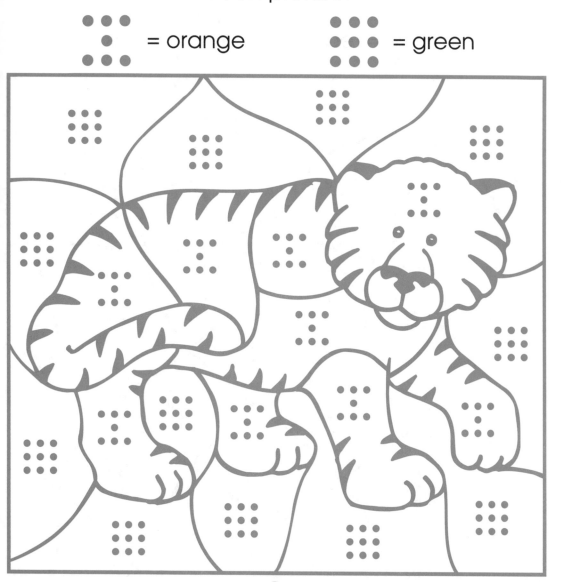

FS109006 • Numbers Hidden Pictures

A Symbol of Love

This shape is seen on Valentine's Day.

Color to find the hidden picture.

= red = pink

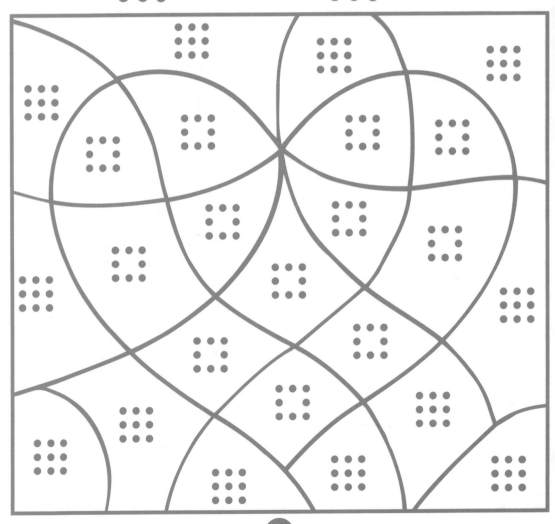

FS109006 • Numbers Hidden Pictures

Flipper

This playful animal lives in the ocean.

Color to find the hidden picture.

= blue

= gray

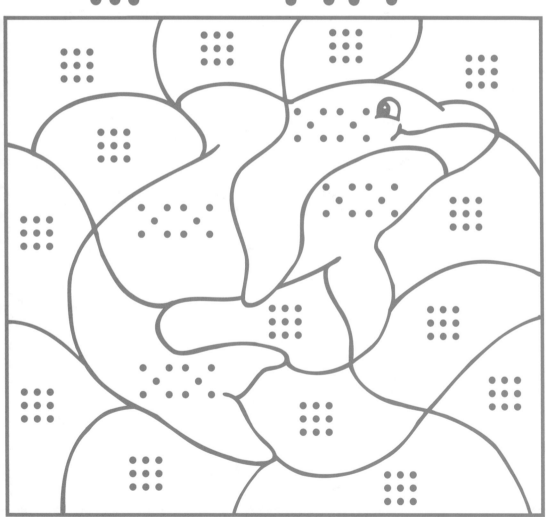

Clowning Around

He makes people laugh and smile.

Color to find the hidden picture.

● = red   ●● = yellow   ●●● = blue

FS109006 • Numbers Hidden Pictures

Catch!

This is fun to bounce and catch.

Color to find the hidden picture.

• • = green   • • • = orange   = yellow

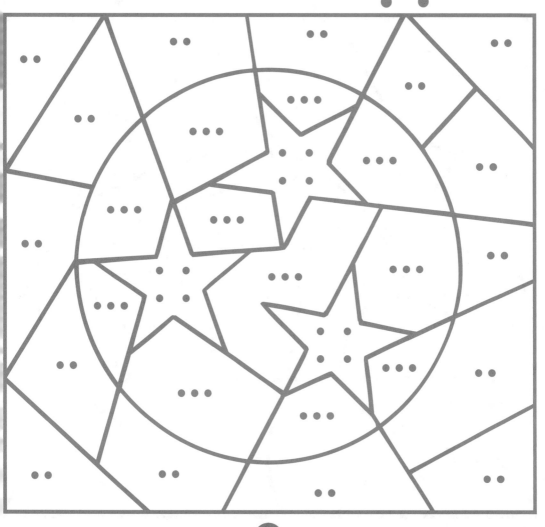

FS109006 • Numbers Hidden Pictures

Let's Race!

This is loud and goes very fast.

Color to find the hidden picture.

● ● ● = black   = yellow   = red

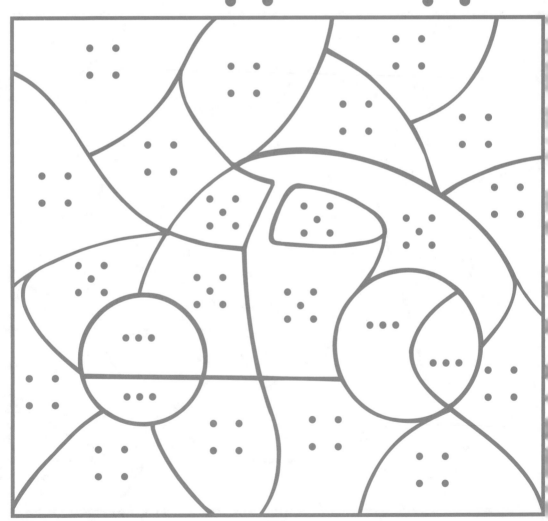

FS109006 • Numbers Hidden Pictures

What a Machine!

This machine can dig and scoop.

Color to find the hidden picture.

= yellow   = black   = blue

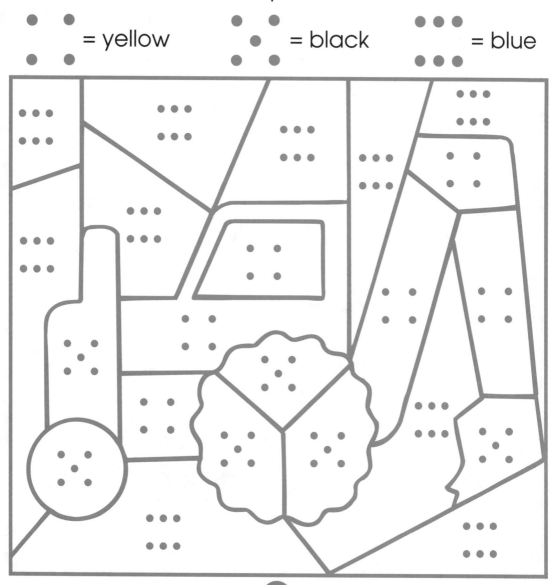

21

Sweet Treat

This little bug makes honey in a hive.

Color to find the hidden picture.

= blue   = black   = yellow

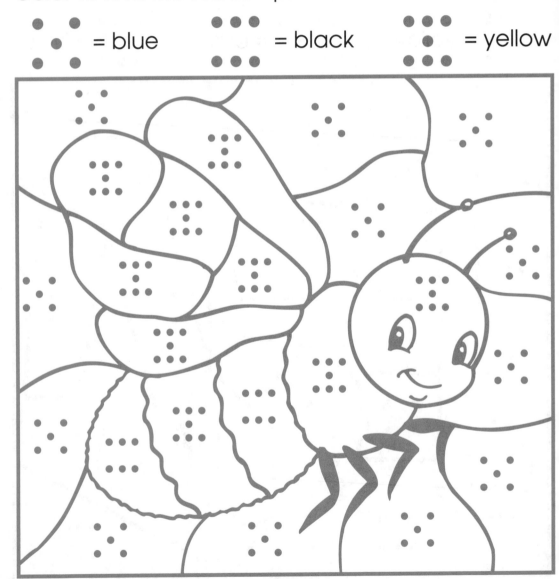

22

So Pretty

This can be seen blooming in the spring.

Color to find the hidden picture.

= blue   = red   = yellow

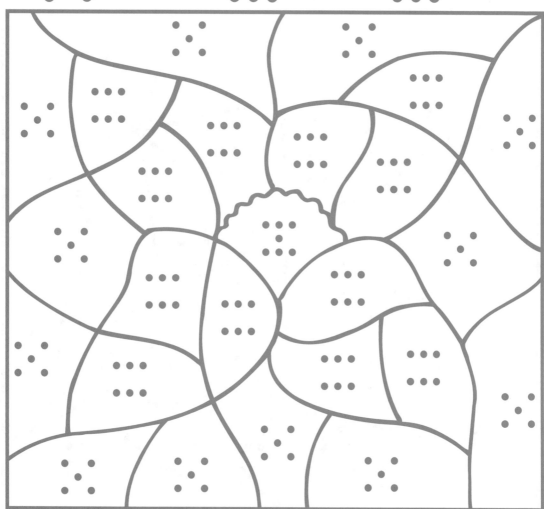

© Carson-Dellosa   FS109006 • Numbers Hidden Pictures

Sky High

This is fun to fly on a windy day.

Color to find the hidden picture.

= orange   = purple   = blue

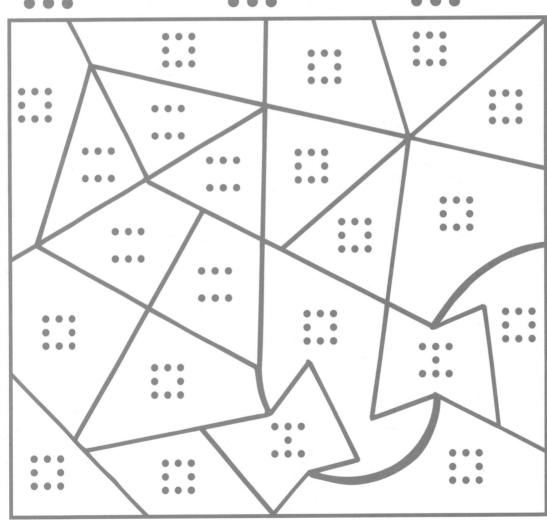

FS109006 • Numbers Hidden Pictures

Beep! Beep!

This can take you on a windy ride.

Color to find the hidden picture.

= red   = blue   = brown

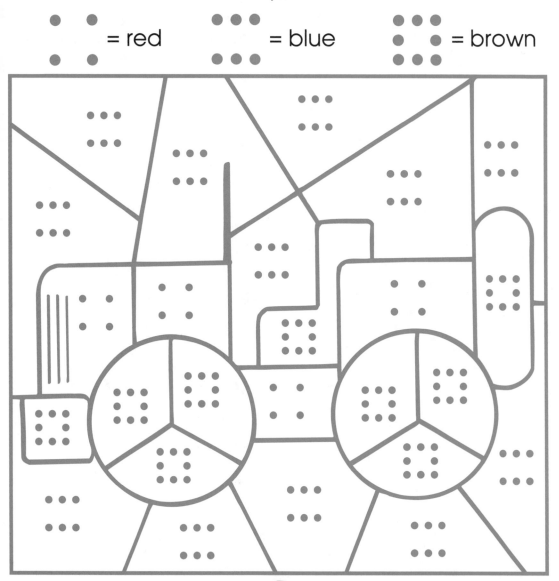

25

Lights On!

This handy tool will help you see in the dark.

Color to find the hidden picture.

= blue   = yellow   = purple

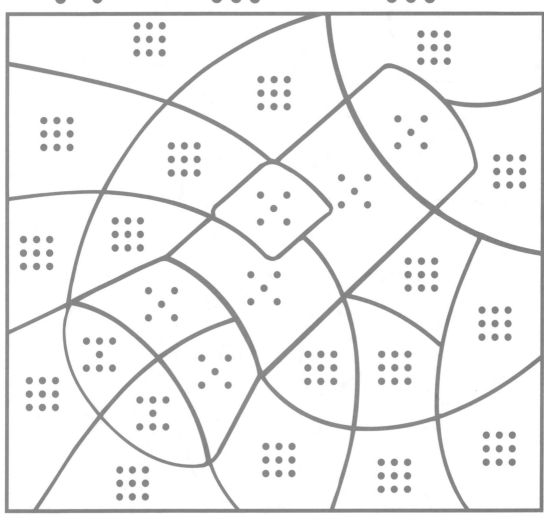

© Carson-Dellosa   FS109006 • Numbers Hidden Pictures

Batter Up!

These things are used in a summer sport.

Color to find the hidden picture.

⠿ = white   ⠿ = brown   ⠿ = green

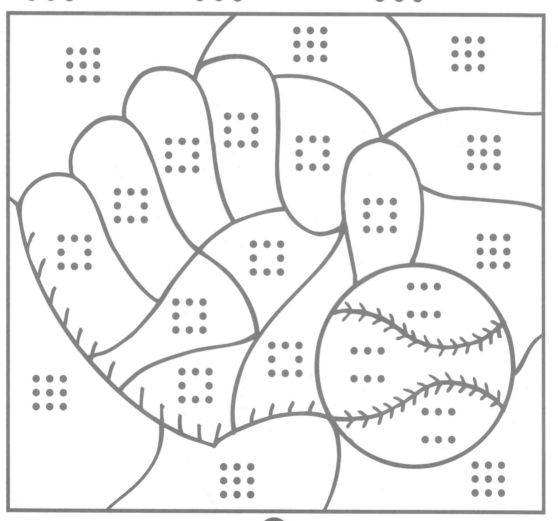

Quack! Quack!

This animal quacks and lives near ponds.

Color to find the hidden picture.

= yellow   = blue   = orange

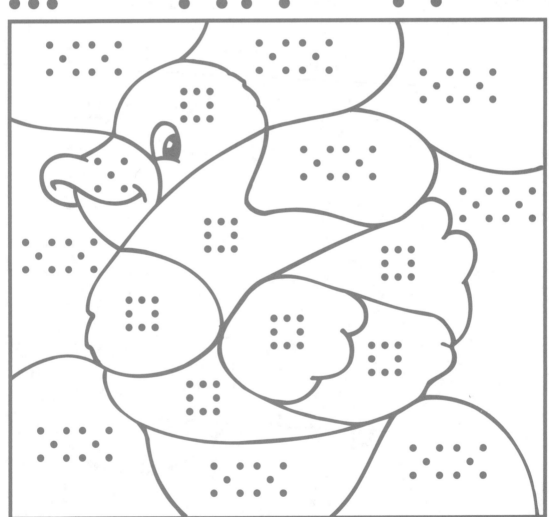

FS109006 • Numbers Hidden Pictures

Watch Out!

Never get too close to one of these!

Color to find the hidden picture.

I = green   2 = yellow

So Cute!

This chubby animal likes to eat bamboo shoots.

Color to find the hidden picture.

2 = black   **3** = green

FS109006 • Numbers Hidden Pictures

Ocean Swimmer

This animal likes to swim in warm water.

Color to find the hidden picture.

3 = gray   **4** = blue

Big and Furry

This animal sleeps a lot in the winter.

Color to find the hidden picture.

4 = brown   5 = green

FS109006 • Numbers Hidden Pictures

A Pesky Pest

You might see this on a picnic.

Color to find the hidden picture.

5 = red   **6** = blue

FS109006 • Numbers Hidden Pictures

Super Shoes

Yee–haw! You might wear these to a rodeo.

Color to find the hidden picture.

6 = green   **7** = blue

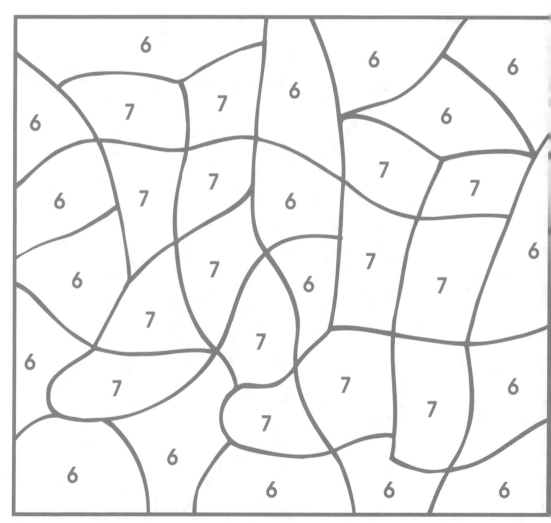

Blow!

This makes a sound that is loud and clear.

Color to find the hidden picture.

7 = orange   **8** = purple

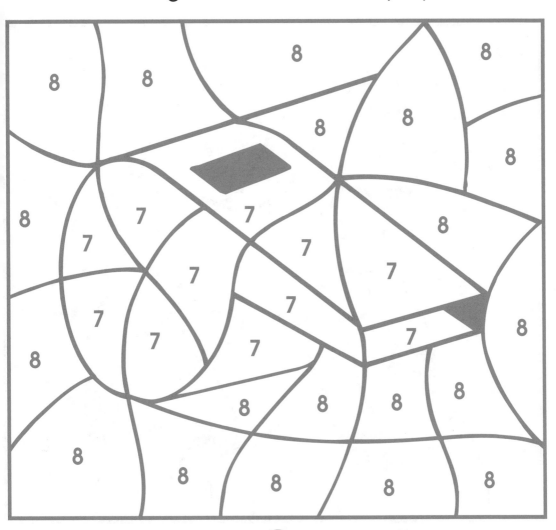

Giddyup!

This animal is fun to saddle up and ride!

Color to find the hidden picture.

8 = yellow   **9** = brown

A Lot of Legs

This little animal has 8 legs!

Color to find the hidden picture.

9 = black   10 = yellow

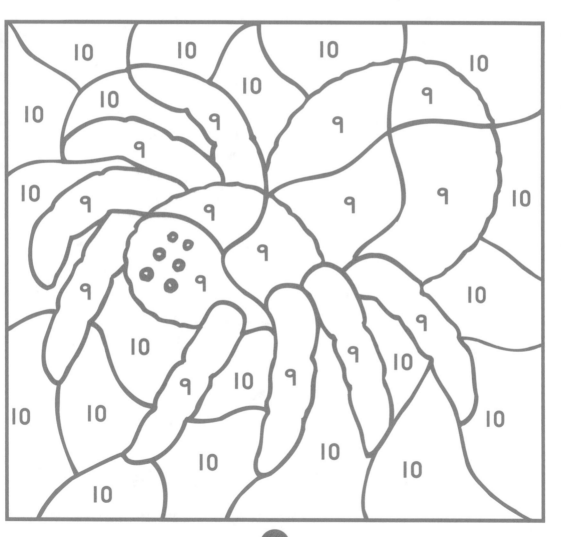

Sky Light

This twinkles in the night sky.

Color to find the hidden picture.

1 = yellow   4 = blue

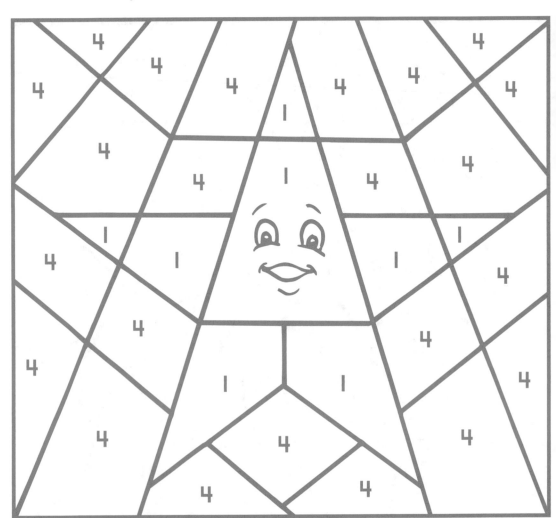

A Big Helper

This helps cars that are broken.

Color to find the hidden picture.

3 = blue   **8** = orange

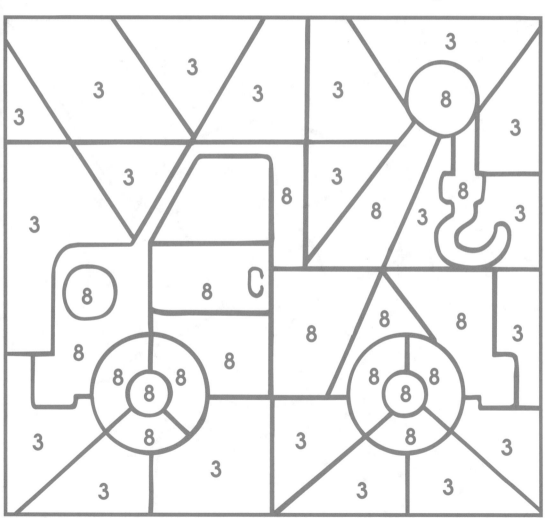

Bright and Yellow

This keeps you warm!

Color to find the hidden picture.

2 = yellow   **5** = orange

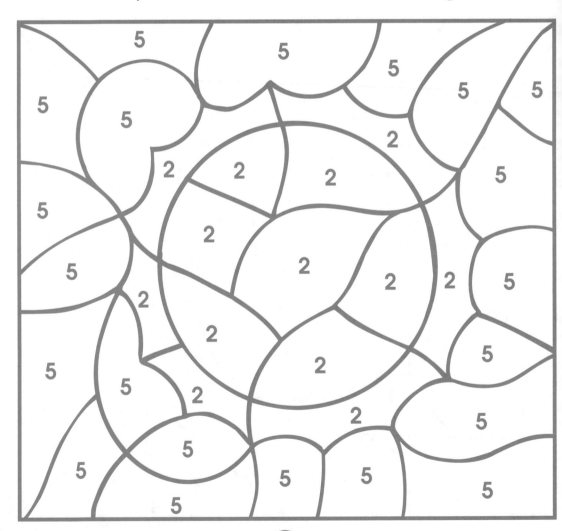

   40

Soft and Furry

This little animal stores nuts for the winter.

Color to find the hidden picture.

4 = gray   9 = green

FS109006 • Numbers Hidden Pictures

A Big Jumper

This animal carries its baby in a pouch.

Color to find the hidden picture.

4 = brown   4 = green

FS109006 • Numbers Hidden Pictures

Load It Up!

You can move dirt easily with this.

Color to find the hidden picture.

6 = green   9 = red

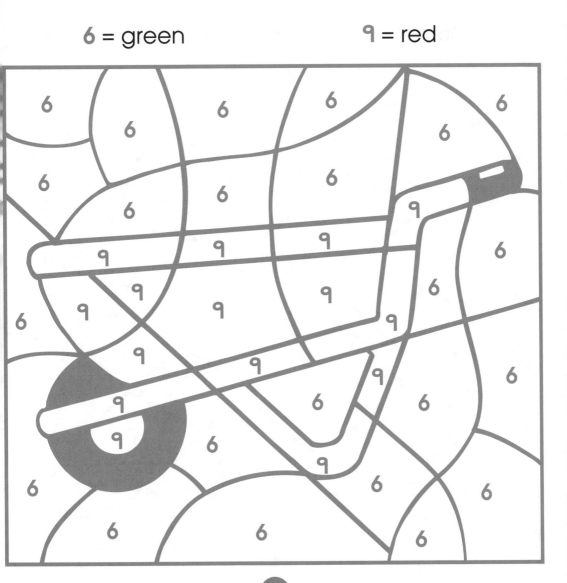

Can This Dragon Fly?

This insect likes to fly near water.

Color to find the hidden picture.

1 = green   **2** = blue   **3** = yellow

Do Not Lose These!

You cannot drive a car without one of these!

Color to find the hidden pictures.

2 = green   **3** = yellow   **4** = blue

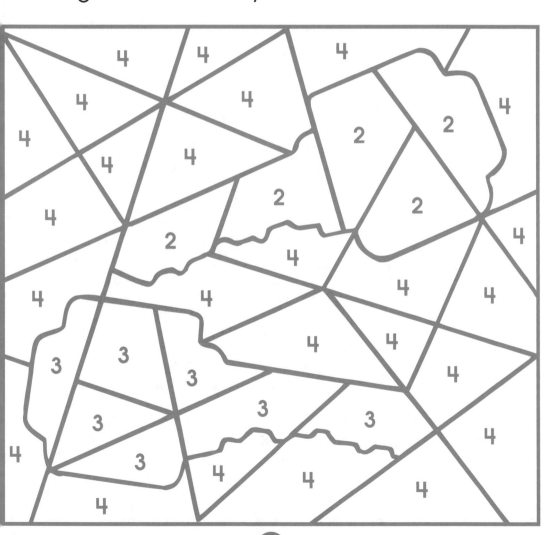

FS109006 • Numbers Hidden Pictures

Strum and Hum

You can make beautiful music with this.

Color to find the hidden picture.

3 = brown   4 = orange   5 = yellow

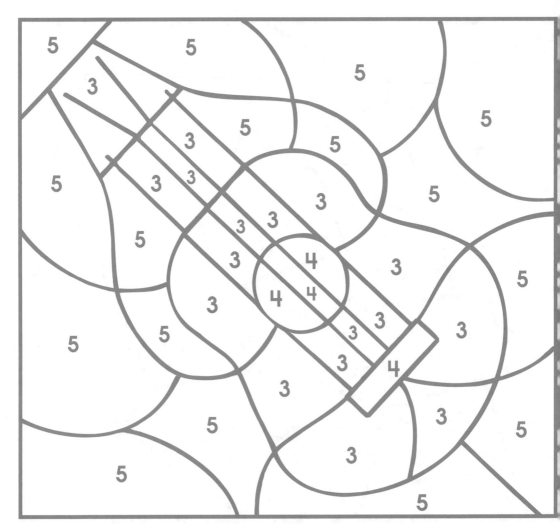

Going Batty

This wide-winged animal likes to fly at night.

Color to find the hidden picture.

5 = black   **6** = brown   **7** = yellow

All Dressed Up

This bird likes to swim!

Color to find the hidden picture.

6 = black   **7** = yellow   **8** = blue

It Will Not Open!

You need a key to open this.

Color to find the hidden picture.

7 = gray   **8** = pink   **9** = yellow

FS109006 • Numbers Hidden Pictures

Cruising Along

This can bounce or jump over waves.

Color to find the hidden picture.

8 = blue   **9** = red   **10** = black

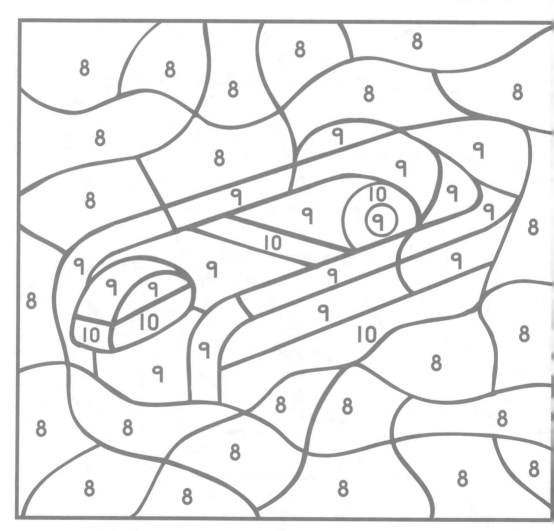

Help for a Farmer

You could see this important machine on a farm.

Color to find the hidden picture.

1 = red   **2** = black   **3** = yellow   **4** = green

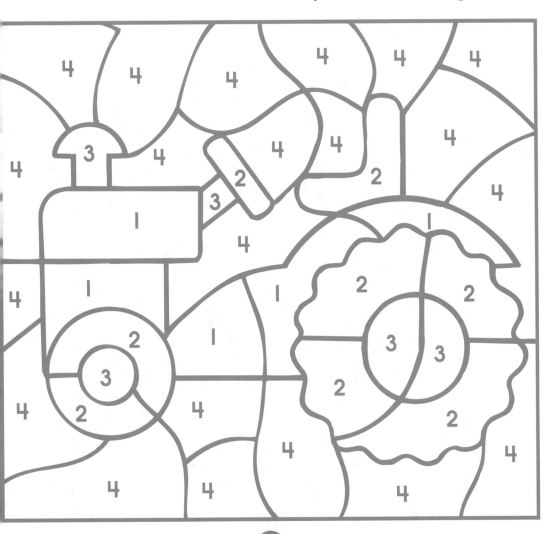

Your Majesty!

This is fit for a king or a queen!

Color to find the hidden picture.

| = green   2 = blue   4 = yellow   7 = red

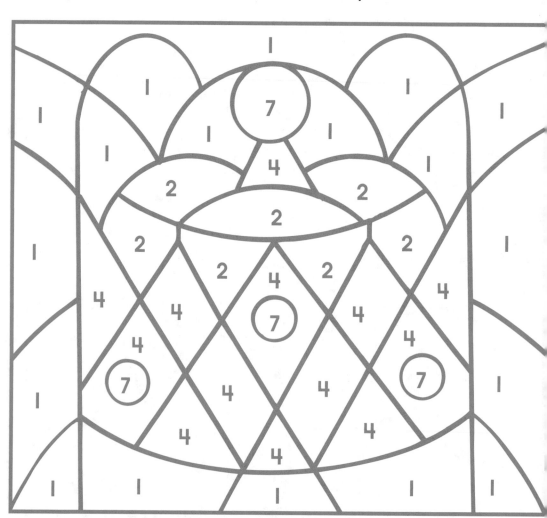

FS109006 • Numbers Hidden Pictures

Polly Want a Cracker?

You might hear this animal talk!

Color to find the hidden picture.

2 = red   **4** = yellow   **6** = blue   **8** = green

FS109006 • Numbers Hidden Pictures

I Can Change!

This little animal can turn into a beautiful butterfly!
Color to find the hidden picture.

3 = brown   **7** = black   **8** = blue   **9** = green

© Carson-Dellosa   54   FS109006 • Numbers Hidden Pictures

Leaping Lizards!

This reptile has a scaly body.

Color to find the hidden picture.

7 = green   **8** = brown   **9** = black   **10** = yellow

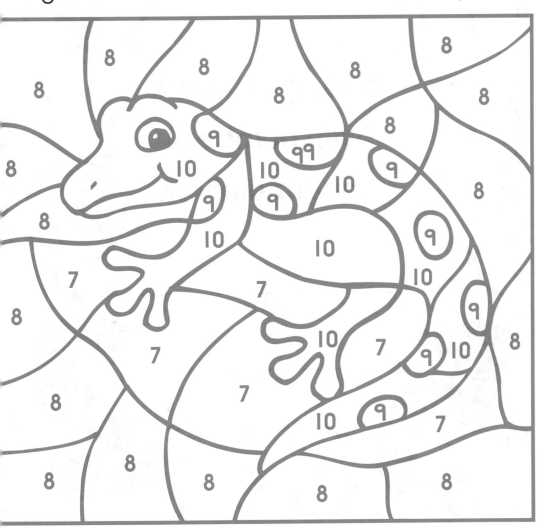

does great work
with numbers!
Congratulations!

_____
signature

_____
date